Mastodon Dentist 30:
Hard Break
Special Edition
With artwork by William D. Hicks

Mastodon Dentist 30: Hard Break is published in the USA by Shoe Music Press, Alpharetta, GA. Its contents are protected by copyright. All Rights reserved by the respective authors.

Mastodon Dentist has appeared in serial under the ISSN: 1947-1440

Thank you to Linda King for her input in making this publication.

Front cover image "Look both ways" by William D. Hicks.

Title Page image "Yellow" by William D. Hicks

A Note by the editor

Poets lead an enchanted life - or at least everything they see, everywhere they go fills them with some sort of enchanted feeling, feelings that lead to remarkable poetry, in spite of our sometimes foggy recollections. Much like a dream state that always involves moving - hardly allowing rest, we traverse time in the hopes that it will reveal some kind of trail and light the path to the future.

The poetry and artwork in this issue marry the natural and manmade worlds in a stunning and colorful way. We hope you enjoy what we have to offer here and may a little bit of it carry with you in your journey.

-Gordon Purkis, editor

Table of Contents

Greg Farnam
In an Unguarded Moment, Fastlane104 Reveals Itself 1
Thank You For Keeping Us Safe. 2
The Heroes Come to the Spam File 3
Taylor Swift and My Ego 4

A.J. Huffman
The Great Escape 5
Of Bullets and Butterflies 7
Corner of Ash and Answer 8

Helen Carey
Still, Life 9
In a Blackout 10
Riverside 13
Prototype 14

Michael Lee Johnson
Busy at Work 16
Jasper 17
Native I Am, Cocopa 18

Roy Bentley
Very Few Roadways 19
After the Gauguins 21

Ian Mullins
The Driver 22

Sonny Traylor
Angry Autumn 24
Symphonies on a Secret Wavelength 26

Dan Encarnacion
Interlude 28
Nurtured 30

David Garyan
Blended Suspended 31
Back Home 32
Under Neon 34
Abrasion 36

Stacy Lynn Mar
When Cigars Fly 37
Only The Young Have Such Moments 38
Boxes 39
An Explanation For The Lonely 40
On the Other Hand 41
Formless 42

Jennifer Ihasz
Sidewalk Etiquette 43
Rushmore 46
Doctor Patient 48

Contributor Bios 49

About the Featured Artist: William D. Hicks is a writer who lives in Chicago, Illinois by himself (any offers?) Contrary to popular belief, he is not related to the famous comedian Bill Hicks (though he's just as funny in his own right). Hicks will someday publish his memoirs, but most likely they will be about Bill Hicks' life. His poetry has appeared in *Outburst Magazine*, *The Legendary, Horizon Magazine, Breadcrumb Sins, Inwood Indiana Literary Magazine, The Short Humour Site* (UK), *The Four Cornered Universe, Save the Last Stall for Me* and *Mosaic*. His art appears in *The Legendary* and as cover art in *Anti-Poetry* and *Sketch*.

"Bridge" by William D. Hicks

Greg Farnum - In an Unguarded Moment, Fastlane104 Reveals Itself

The magazines promised to take me inside Adele's world.
It was the big box store.
I had stopped in to listen to the In-Store Broadcasting Network,
it was giving me helpful diet tips.
Excited pixels invited my purchase.
I obeyed the command to enter my PIN number
"I'm from the future" I told Fastlane104,
"Me too" it replied.
Outside on the vast concrete plain of the parking lot
a cold rain had swept in.

Greg Farnum - Thank You For Keeping Us Safe.

It came too late for Pontiac,
once a City, now stripped bare,
you came too late for keeping it safe;
and even a busy corner like this one,
Walton and Baldwin, could no longer sustain
the popular provider of chicken-like substance,
fried in a tasty spicy finger lickin' batter,
and across the street at VG's supermarket
the residents shuffle in, or scrounge for empties
in the garbage cans out front,
poorer now than they were last year,
and poorer then than the year before
but still wracking up VG customer reward points
and never seeming to complain
as they lead their life-like existence
...or do they? What do you hear
o secret electronic ear? Do they murmur
in their sleep, these guys in old ill-fitting flannel shirts?
Or the poorly dressed women,
poorly dressed though Bangladeshis have died
to ensure that every American has
the cheapest clothes possible
—too poor for that?
Do they complain as they shuffle through the store?
Do they complain great ear to the sky?
And the chickens,
do they complain while they are being
turned into science fiction?
What do you hear?
Noise?
Info?

Chatter?

Keep us safe.

Greg Farnum - The Heroes Come to the Spam File

More heroes had come home. I was deeper in debt.
And then to the spam file:
Dog food coupon revolution.
The matter of each moment,
its ticking content in the book of life.
Nazi bride murder...
Rat meat sold...
Disturbing stats on war vets
Israeli missiles strike again
Miley Cyrus: I'm no.1 on Maxim's Hot List
Cyber everything
At the door,
the wolf.

Greg Farnum - Taylor Swift and My Ego

    ram air

          critics weigh in

mini guide

The day begins
(again)
(it hasn't failed me yet)
via e-mail?
No, for real
—too long at this screen
and the day has just begun. . .
      Taylor Swift – that is my message
for the day as my horoscope warns
Egocentric power plays are a no-no.
Don't worry, my ego is dissolving in a digital flood
Taylor Swift.

"Aerial Tram View" by William D. Hicks

A.J. Huffman - The Great Escape

is a duplicitous dual of semantics.
Which came first? The chicken believes
the egg is cracked, but still waivers
when it reads molecular science textbooks,
ponders the Big Bang Theory. The egg
always remains reticent, knows its time
table is tenuous at best, forgives the chicken
its ego, even as another beak shatters its world.

"Lake Weed 2" by William D. Hicks

A.J. Huffman - Of Bullets and Butterflies

The firing of silver
iridescence launches flight
from finger. One from perch,
one from point. Both a beautiful blur
of disengaged perspective. Wings
whine against trajectory, look for
resistance to cut. Forward
is the force of evolution, erupting
in an array of breathing color,
spotting the world with red.

A.J. Huffman - Corner of Ash and Answer

is a false fable, a pipe-dream of princesses
and fairy godmothers that grant wishes, gift
wrap prince charmings with magical ballgowns
and delicate glass slippers. In reality, it is just
a bigger house with more corners to sweep,
another mouth to feed, more clothes to pick up.
The dress is yellowing in the attic, right
next to her life's ambitions, any form
of independence she ever longed for,
and that bastard clock that chimes twelve, twice
a day, a constant reminder to be
careful what you ask for.

Helen Carey - Still, Life

Left unattended, the after-work
silt of the day curls into itself
slowly, my legs curl into yours
and Hopper's light droops
across Washington Square,
designating the space between
this summer and next, the moon
flowers at the end of the season
and the tinny feel of sobriety
on colder mornings.

Hours along with the rest
of the perennials freeze
over slowly, the fire
escape garden a shadow
box of the past two years.

But in the subway the smell
of rosemary on my fingers
makes this whole city swim
like the inside of a cell and
you walk to work through
someone else's Tuesday,
taking inventory on leftover
logic and counting down
the days until last season,
weeks chiming against
my knuckles like bells.

Helen Carey - In a Blackout

Even in this season's
shallow breath, days steep
at the end of weeks, the sound
of their slow shuffling along
the stars lasting for miles.

But the taste of another
April on another's
tongue goes unnoticed
in such agreeable air,
and the distance between
myself and the fact of
being human practically
widens on command—

The slow-moving
dialects of our nights
now rivaled only by
those of my words, dangling
like thousands of pull-strings
waiting to be tugged
across all of my unlit days.

"Traffic" by William D. Hicks

"Graveyard" by William D. Hicks

Helen Carey - Riverside

Even at our most mundane,
images sputter calmly
back to us—less deterred
by the present than we are,
they hang like Spanish moss
over long mornings, lie
in wait for years under
downturned brows.

Eye-level with water
towers ten floors above
the city, and there's the white
church again at the end
of a sandy graveyard
and three baby raccoons
at the top of a tree,
staring down at you.

So when the white
of the eye at the back of
the mind pauses between
the pictures, you wake like
a tourist to your own life
and can almost hear
the ticking of your own heart
into the deep space outside it,
where you came from.

Helen Carey - Prototype

Once fall sifted through
summer, our light turned
murky, sides of houses
and tops of trees swam
in a glow half-nauseating.

When we were young
we knelt beside the season,
capsized. Life still billowed
above us then, like a sheet
lifted in the air by
older hands before sleep—
a show of comfort
against watered down days.

When our hands
become the older ones,
do we swell the air
above younger sorrows
or simply create heat?

"Parking Lot" by William D. Hicks

Michael Lee Johnson - Busy at Work

Busy at work,
after the bad news:
memo: "your daughter died"—
I see her words
scattered in silent
tears,
scribbled
over the desk
top calendar,
partially dried.

Michael Lee Johnson - Jasper

In an attic
the size of a
single bed,
Jasper, 89, simple life,
dips his Oreo cookie
in moist oatmeal and milk.
Six months ago
his driver's license
Expired—
between the onset
of macular degeneration
and gas at $4.65 a gallon,
life for Jasper has stalled out
in the middle lane
like his middle of the month
social security check, it's gone.
There's nothing academic about Jasper's life.
Today, the journey is the stepping stairs
spiraling downward to the mailbox
in the corridor area.
Midway, he leans against the cool
walls for breath with his oxygen tank,
no rails to hang on to.
The Chicago Cubs are playing on the radio,
and Jasper reaches for his cigarettes
in his top left pocket.

Michael Lee Johnson - Native I Am, Cocopa

Now once great events fading
into seamless history,
I am mother proud.
My native numbers are few.
In my heart digs many memories
forty-one relatives left in1937.
Decay is all left of their bones, memories.
I pinch my dark skin.
I dig earthworms
farm dirt from my fingertips
grab native
Baja and Southwestern California,
its soil and sand wedged between my spaced teeth.
I see the dancing prayers of many gods.
I am Cocopa, remnants of Yuman family.
I extend my mouth into forest fires
Colorado rivers, trout filled mountain streams.
I survive on corn, melons, and
pumpkins, mesquite beans.
I still dance in grass skirts
drink a hint of red Sonora wine.

I am mother proud.
I am parchment from animal earth.

Roy Bentley - Very Few Roadways

The tire was huge. And black. And about as round
as the suddenly-open mouth of someone screaming.
In my case I may have thought, *Very few roadways
offer protection against the rogue tire loosed and
bounding down from nowhere to cross the median.*
It's the same when a terrible dream you wake from
is the quiet and stillness after a near-fatal accident
in which you walk away distrusting deliverance.
In my case, I believed that I'd been killed. Died

on an interstate outside a town in West Virginia.
At impact, I'd seen lots of frozen instants inching
toward joy—the births of screaming grandchildren,
completion of certain arduous tasks involving years
of personal sacrifice and skilled attention. There is
death and grave injury. And of course the Mystery.
A blackness looming like some great truck tire—
*the Puncture-Sealing Tire For Rugged Off-Road
Conditions Like Coal Fields: the G177 DuraSeal—*

in the split-second it bounce-bounces toward you.
This was like that. And like nothing else. I saw
the face of my passenger-daughter, her mouth
frozen into a wide *O* of fear. Which of course is
the ah-hah shock of recognition at what's coming
like a visitation you can never quite prepare for.
Like the child who asks the conductor where
the train is stopping next and is told "up ahead"
and repeats that as if he's naming a new town.

"Tree" by William D. Hicks

Roy Bentley - After the Gauguins

Each was married to someone else and saw things as not
being paradise or perdition but about what you might expect.

She liked sitting quietly for an hour and asked him to travel
to the National Gallery. She wanted him to see that women

in the paintings of Paul Gauguin all have downcast eyes
but no shame. Like butterflies, they have flitted about

before alighting by fires—their black manes driving
the play of flame, at least one scrawny yellow dog

to guard smoke making the glyph for an afterlife.
Who needs the cargo of deliberate ships from Paris

if you're catching sight of Enchantment, deciphering
the codes of existence in blossoming breadfruit trees?

Afterwards, waiting for the metro, he looked down.
Beside the rail, a fat rat the ash-grey color of the skies

where she would be moving for work soon, without him.
After the National Gallery, the Gauguins, he could look

at a rat and glimpse most of what the foreseeable future
comes whizzing through without message or meaning.

Ian Mullins - The Driver

I tell you, that beautiful angry mob
ripped the car
like it was last year's dress;

would have shredded his skin
like paper, plucked eyeballs
from his head
but there he was, seventies superstar
with more make-up on his face
than any of the girls out there,
sitting on the back seat of the car
boa like a polecat
striped round his neck,
golden tear silvered in his cheek
like a shard of broken glass
and smiling
like he's just been elected;

and I remember this one face
smeared on the window like breath
on a fish-tank
wondering how he could breathe
the air in there
and how she could maybe breathe some herself

all he did
you know what he did
he touched two fingers to his lips
and kissed the mouth lip-sticked on the glass
and god-damn, that girl's face
broke open like an egg
with two yolks
her smile could have parted the red sea

but she was taken
by the undertow, spun out into the crowd
like a wild flower dropped
into a waterfall

maybe she's still spinning now;
maybe each new kiss tastes of sunlight
on glass
each new lover has a tear on his cheek

Sonny Traylor - Angry Autumn

The last of the
rust colored leaves
finally let go, and
the furious trees flail
their skeleton branches
as if trying to pluck
a hapless angel
from the heavens.

"Winter Willows 5" by William D. Hicks

Sonny Traylor - Symphonies on a Secret Wavelength

Clouds roll in out of the west,
Shape shifters dancing
An ancient pantomime.

The fish becomes a fox,
The fox becomes a face,
The face is frowning,
But the rain is not tears.
The rain is just rain,
And the people are just people
On their morning commute.

Caffeine instead of souls
They coax their bones
Into cubicles,
They slog to assembly lines,
Never hearing the symphonies
Ripple through the puddles
That are all around them.

"Rainy Door" by William D. Hicks

Dan Encarnacion - Interlude
after Edward Hopper's *Chop Suey*

Empty out your purse, she had asked of the woman sitting opposite across
The day-bathed café table—whose tensed charcoal back surfaces our faces.
She had asked, *Is your name the same as mine?* The back-faced woman's
Eyes had slipped out the wide third floor window that egged in the warm
Low slung saffron sunlight—the back-faced woman had seen three letters
(Not SOS, not DOA, not POW, not MIA, not enc, not RCA, not RKO, nor REO)
Framed through the pane unlit on the large red vertical transparent-bulbed
Sign outside. "My name is Sue." She'd then said again, *Empty out your purse,*
Adding in, *Please humor me.* The back-faced woman—her deportment, guise
Of dress as youthful and modish (slim simple frock of combed-probably-wool
To ward off chill from the asserting autumn air, bobbed hair, undistinguished
Indistinguishable tight head-hugging hat) as the other's who faces full-faced
Toward us—looks up at the front-faced woman whose head crooks narrowed

Contemplation quiet when seen from a distance (or in a bad reproduction), but
Step right up to these two women and you will see she is eyeing the back-faced
Woman's brow for candor. The back-faced woman has asked, "Is it necessary?"
The front-faced woman has replied, *How much simulacrum may be contained*?
Hunched forward, as if divulging a secret or petitioning confidence, the back-
Faced woman brokenly speaks subdued syllables while focusing on her unseen
Tea bowl. The women have yet to pour the tea. Or, they have finished it off
Under pantomimed pretense of advocacy for sociability, or bladed discomfort.
Empty your purse, please. The back-faced woman dumps its contents (lotion,
Lipstick, lighter, Life Savers, a compact, condoms, Turkish cigarettes, cigarette
Holder, phone book, fountain pen, gloves, earrings, billfold, scattered change,
A pillbox filled with cocaine, a copy of *The Communist Manifesto*). The front-
Faced woman quickly quantifies and qualifies the spread objects, then shoves

Them far to one side. She opens and overturns her own purse (lotion, lipstick,
Lighter, Wrigley's Doublemint, a compact, Turkish cigarettes, cigarette holder,
Gloves, earrings, billfold, scattered change, a pillbox filled with cocaine, a torn
Copy of *This Side of Paradise*). The back-faced woman indicates, "You haven't
A phone book nor condoms." The front-faced woman states, *I have no use for*
A phone book nor condoms. There are other methods. The back-faced woman
Wads her handkerchief, "I didn't know what to do with him." Across the table
Is said, *Yet you insulated him.* We assume she speaks—can't see her lips move,
"He stole me. Like that man who's not hearing that woman speaking to him at

The table by the other window, he absorbs everything, but does not give back."
My heart strings go ping. "If he were with us, all the light would shine on him."
This would not have happened had you not taken him from me. "I know myself,
But that is all."

Dan Encarnacion - Nurtured

"The monster is nothing more than
the invention of his victims."
        - Kobo Abe, *The Face of Another*

Will smile. Will whistle licentiously. Will rise
Early—most mornings—erect, ready to roam.
A rush of red spread across his cheeks, crooked

Childish teeth. Your mouth would water should
You spy to see him sour with each untempered
Crunch. He likes his apples green and polished

To shine back the sky. He was a boy. He is indubitably
A boy. Will hover with angled wings. Will feather
The rooks with rocks—a workman's full handful.

Will manhandle the books. Will deliver his grandma
To church. Will lunch alone. Will oil old cars.
Will outswim the sun at the cusp of dusk. Will spout

His name and, as his face, you'll find it unremarkable
As a boot. A brain paved with rain-wet gray—a disused
Back alley. His hair a crib for debilitated deliberation-smoke.
The sheriff referred to him as *full of spunk*. The gym
Teacher agreed, said *though he was skinny, the ropes
He shimmied* with ease; *that boy sure got grit. He was*

A boy. Climbed trees in the orchard to crunch through
Fruit and hide when he wondered why he flushed red
When boys would flock to flirt with girls. Masked

By the topmost branches, he hung to ripen. Though hung
Was the jury, hung was the man who asked for a smoke
At the interstate rest-stop where the two had crossed
Passions and entwined to duel under shadow of shame.

David Garyan - Blended Suspended

Through barefaced hills she led me,
where unhinged rocks scraped
against the thin patches of her shoes
and scraps of sagebrush lay
scattered around narrow switchbacks.

I shivered in sugarcoated heat as the
black ink began dripping from her sable hair,
and the pulseless breeze
sang with afternoon's volatile sunbeams.

Her voice sounded like a detuned violin,
and she offered no answers to my questions
when her susurrus words dissolved
in my constricted ears.

Slowly we reached the newborn summit,
where she laid her illuminated body
against glowing swords of trembling grass,
and asked me to pour my remaining
water onto her shapeshifting face.

David Garyan - Back Home

I stare at the laughing rain
from my homesick window,
wondering whether there
are enough roofs tonight,
I want to go out and
count the sedating chimneys of
abstinent bars,
cradling your sinking spirit
with wet blankets,
will you be cold when
the doors finally close?
will I catch you stalking
the mourning shadows
cast by late night
convenience stores?

"Lampost" by William D. Hicks

David Garyan - Under Neon

Oh, tobacco bathed busker,
where is your bed tonight?
amongst yawning lights
that wither on vigilant avenues
I watched you exorcise
morose chords from a guitar
with no strings.

Do you hear those shivering sounds?
do you feel these newspaper blankets
and concrete pillows soaking in
your kerosene drenched hair while
carnivorous traffic
feasts on your dreams?

Tonight, I will walk by again
and drop a few more coins in your humble basket,
wishing that you would
jump on those wheezing locomotives
and visit ghost towns
of perpetual sleep.

"Goodrich Rubbers" by William D. Hicks

David Garyan - Abrasion

Careworn friends tread
past seaside benches
on the splintering boardwalk,
where yesterday's woolgatherers
recede against the fatigued sunset
of sleepless dreams,
and the tattered, inaccessible pier
hugs every lubricated wave
anointed by distant oil tankers,
but when seraphic darkness calls,
people gather around the fire pit
to drink the fermented flames of hope.

Stacy Lynn Mar - When Cigars Fly

The evening is as silent
As an overcast sky,
Undertone crackling of
Unearthed thunder,
Voice of the God's
Marble in their statues,
Aphrodite in her sea
Of red hearts
And all I find
In the essence of all this mess
is a box of cigars,
Each posed with white wings
Ready to fly
Out into the eye of
This night's wide storm,
Away from wide mouths
Forming hollow o's
To the 'no' that drops
From hungry lips,
Nicotine-flavored
And lying, lying
Just to die
When they say,
'this is the last time.'

Stacy Lynn Mar - Only The Young Have Such Moments

The girl is leaning close to the boy's face,
Is telling him why objects lost from
The soft hands of strangers
Are really heirlooms disguised as garbage.
She holds a matchbox toward his face,
Delicately, the cardboard glowing
Of acrylic paint and super-glued lace.
Tells him it's a concubine for one lonely heart,
The slippery paper taped to the corner
Once held a doughnut which touched
The lips of a young boy's first kiss.
She says she likes to paste and rearrange
otherwise insignificant pieces of people's lives,
The smell of Japanese take-out
On the sixth Sabbath, fortunes unsnapped
From cookies and still smelling of sugar.
Says she is stealing memories,
Making those lost, semi-witnessed moments
Immortal in their own rights.
He listens, one eye trained against the sky,
Sinking beneath the dark holes
The stars form in their broken constellations.
He is dreaming of their first kiss
And how she might savor it,
All the while she's recalling the strange smile
Of John Lennon on the cover of a vintage record,
Wondering how she can illuminate
The vinyl in a decoupage-styled collage
without losing the infinite kiss of Yoko Ono.

Stacy Lynn Mar - Boxes

The thought is almost implausible,
How definitive a word 'goodbye'
Can sound in a room empty, spare
The marble floors and corduroy upholstery.
The stars outside the window
Transpire, that tribe of diamond flash
And gleaming atmospheric dust,
The wind tap-dancing tree branches,
Through each open window
Where the moon is spinning his steady glow
Into our theatric interpretation of separation.
How insecure they seem, and us both
In those arthritic, winding morning hours,
Clocks of the world spending their seconds,
Lovers unfolding, sewing, unhinging like doors.
You are as substantial as a sugar bowl,
The salt on brie, an aesthetic eyeball,
Yet all I see are the boxes,
Rectangular, brown, white, plastic crates
Patiently awaiting in one spine crack
To their cardboard backs, to take you away.

Stacy Lynn Mar - An Explanation For The Lonely

The moon carried a little flame,
spectator of taillights at dusk.
In front of my house I gathered the boys
like little jars of sex
the elements of true lovers
and a magic with two birthdays.
Love sat in my heart like a fever,
the low point of my body
a servant I did not love
with its forgiven colors and pretend silks.
Childhood was my tangled inverse of loud coughs
immortal in the corner of a lit candle
until enough flame could be undone by you.
I gave up other bodies in their tangled sheets
when the moon could no longer hide the latitude
coloring the streets a final closing of doves and owls,
where a frozen door filled the east of
a deep apology for personal longing gone dim.
I loved the fail of our low point
because winter blew you open
like a cold stone of the south,
the days when change lined the living room
till I gave up what was blank.
You became the personal water
to a kind of river where the flow grows in agitation
and flies away in the way of magic
like the opposite of whole swimming west
would invariably equal what you were to me:
true love ailing like a long flu, set as free as
loose sugar caught on the wing of the wind.

Stacy Lynn Mar - On The Other Hand

Her smile was as bright
as the most piercing
of sun-stretched day light,
an overhead screen
for which one's worries
could display before they fade.

She was a southern belle
so beautiful that even
the sky would wonder
if each birth of star
weren't just an iced nail
for which her dreams would hang.

The gentle enlightenment
of an old lady's stare
where you'd debate what
rumination lay behind tired eyes,
sagging at the corners
though still dancing
as forward was the only step she knew.

Even amidst the throws
of anger, as she sometimes was
over fried potatoes
or the moonshine smell
of her third husband,
her smile was as mythical
and broad as a moon stream.
And the sky used to wonder
the strength she had to hold it up.

Stacy Lynn Mar - Formless

She dances wildly,
a slick, black cat caught in space.
There is no form,
only the gentle, rhythmic folding
of arms over torso,
torso over legs,
two feet lost to the samba.
She's a Spanish declaration
you can't translate and besides
it's too late to put your
hands in your pockets,
though they tell lies and
you can't walk without
your legs being in the way.
Her whip of brown hair is flowing
like a quick, chocolate wave
you could ride across
or lick when no one's looking,
except everyone is.

Jennifer Ihasz - Sidewalk Etiquette

Under the last of the light
and the early cast of evening shadows
I halt my passage.
There are two men before me
shuffle-stilled, encased in frayed, old man
saggy-pants and
separated by half a league.
The street was to the right of them
the cemetery to the left;
each has paused
bearing the leashes of their tiny steeds
unfurled but fettered,
still allowing for the two
furry surrogates to
wobble and strain,
one, a chubby little wiener dog
the other
some unknown breed
an elegant sausage in
his furry little sweater.
Each man squints, staring and serious.
I know not what one has done to offend the other
what unknown, invisible, unforgivable slight has
passed—
perhaps one's dog pooped
in the other's polyanthus.
They were washed out, these men,
worked over and faded—
I was close enough to see
their missing buttons,
belts, punched and pulled, cinched
as if what was once robust, well-fed
now let lonely hunger
shear weight from their existence.
One began to work his lips
over a suspiciously toothy mouth,

(Continued on page 44)

I leaned closer to hear what he would say,
but it was nothing.
Both men yanked their leashes and
their two hulks, creaking,
managed to pass each other.
All that was left in their retrospect
were the dug-out spots and misplaced rocks
where two eager dogs had
scrabbled and storm'd
if only to catch the scent
of each other's nether regions
to say a simple "hello"
or to understand where each may have been.

"Street Scene" by William D. Hicks

Jennifer Ihasz - Rushmore

Through the dying ribbon of light
The day is escaping
I can see my father's face
In the ever widening arm of dusk
My mother must have asked me to summon him
To call him inside
For dinner, because she was worried
Because he was neglecting something
I hesitated
Seeing him there
Softened and pinked
By some trick of this light
Or the heat of too much whiskey.
I know between our faces
Something is close
Some similarities.
Between us there were similarities.
Now I wonder how much of that
Is really us
And how much I leached in from the atmosphere.
Is anything ever carved in stone
As you crawl through your timeline
And struggle
How easily will you fit into
The snug vacancy
Left by someone who went before you
Because for all its flaws
It fits
And it's comforting
Like the warm glow of booze
or finding the message
in the ice at the bottom of the glass.

"Go this way" by William D. Hicks

Jennifer Ihasz - Doctor Patient

Heavy
the air is heavy here
it has some solvent ratio
of pain to forgiveness
slowly being turned to poison
and cycled through the lungs.
People lay, limp and dangerous
In danger
the clock quivers
in the pretend atmosphere.
There is passion in something broken
In the velvety synapse
Unchained.
One can hardly be held responsible
If you are attracted to what is flushed
And curved,
calling you to become
Some fleshy cartographer
to truly know someone
deeper than the bone.

Contributor Bios

Greg Farnum has been a soldier, factory worker, ad executive, editor, and (following one of the many recessions) a pizza deliveryman, finding time to write *Doctor's Testament*, a collection of poetry; *The Event*, a novel; *The Pizza Diaries*, a memoir; and *The Celestial Railroad*, an experimental narrative. He is currently at work on a new novel, *Farther Than I Thought*.

Roy Bentley has won fellowships from the National Endowment for the Arts, the Florida Division of Cultural Affairs, and the Ohio Arts Council. He has published three books: *Boy in a Boat* was published by the University of Alabama Press, *Any One Man* by Bottom Dog Books in Huron, Ohio; and a third, *The Trouble with a Short Horse in Montana*, won the White Pine Press poetry award. *Starlight Taxi*, a fourth book, received the 2012 Blue Lynx Prize in Poetry and will be published by *Lynx House* in September.

Helen Carey is a recent college graduate working at a publishing company in New York City. Prior to this, she worked as a copyeditor at a chain of local newspapers in New Jersey, and also held an internship at the PEN American Center in New York. She draws inspiration from a variety of artists, writers, and thinkers – Frank O'Hara to Willa Cather, De Kooning to Krishnamurti, Chaplin to Bob Dylan. Through her writing, she aims to show the beauty in the simple, the mundane, and the ugly.

Dan Encarnacion earned an MFA in Writing at the California College of Arts and lives in Portland, Oregon where he co-curates the *Verse In Person* poetry series. The bleak of Bela Tarr, the spare of Supersilent, and the spike of quad-lattes will palpitate his palpus. Dan has been published in *MARGIE, The Berkeley Review, and/or, Eleven Eleven, SPLIT* and *The Exquisite*

Corpse and elsewhere. His poem "Aposiopesis" was nominated for the 2014 Pushcart Prize.

David Garyan attended Cal State Northridge and has appeared in *Eclipse*, *Mastodon Dentist*, *The Northridge Review* and *Penny Ante Feud*. He currently resides in the Los Angeles area.

A.J. Huffman is a poet and freelance writer in Daytona Beach, Florida. She has previously published six collections of poetry all available on Amazon.com. She has also published her work in numerous national and international literary journals. She is currently the editor for six online poetry journals for *Kind of a Hurricane Press*.

Jennifer Ihasz is a mom and a born-again college student. She is currently studying History and English Literature. When not doing class work she loves to write. She also loves to bore her very loving family with long talks about the finer points of WW II.

Michael Lee Johnson lived for ten years in Canada during the Vietnam era. Today he is a poet, freelance writer, photographer, and small business owner in Itasca, Illinois, who has been published in more than 750 small press magazines in twenty-five countries. He edits seven poetry sites. Michael has released The *Lost American: From Exile to Freedom (136 page book)*, several chapbooks of his poetry, including *From Which Place the Morning Rises* and *Challenge of Night and Day, and Chicago Poems*. He also has over 65 poetry videos on YouTube.

Stacy Lynn Mar is a thirty-something professed bibliophile. She considers herself a creature of the night, preferring the anonymity of smoky bars and dim-lit cafes for her inspiration, though she's partial to brown eyes and the rusty strum of old guitar strings. She lives and writes in a tiny little town in Kentucky.

Ian Mullins was born in Liverpool, England. His e-chapbook *The Dog Outside The Palace Gates* can be read -online. He has published poems in *Purple Patch*, *Off The Coast*, *The Journal*, *Gutter Eloquence*, and many more magazines and websites. His first-published horror story can be read online at the *Black Petals* website.

Sonny Traylor works as a longshoreman on the Lake Erie Port of Cleveland. Some of his work has appeared in *Jersey Devil Press*, *Robot Melon*, and *The Germ*.